Hell:

The Waiting Place of the Dead

Luca Welch

DISPENSATIONAL
PUBLISHING HOUSE, INC.

DISPENSATIONAL PUBLISHING HOUSE
Taos, New Mexico

Hell:
The Waiting Place of the Dead
ISBN: 978-1-961110-41-0

All Scriptures are quoted from the King James Version (KJV).

Dispensational Publishing House, Inc.
P.O. Box 3181
Taos, NM 87571
www.DispensationalPublishing.com

Ordering Information: Quantity sales. Special discounts are available on quantity purchases by churches, associations, and others. For details, contact the publisher at the address above or by phone at 1-844-321-4202.

Printed in the United States of America

CONTENTS

1   Why Study Hell?   1

2   The First Mentions   3

3   All the Dead Went to Sheol   7

4   Sheol / Hades: A Dual Realm   11

5   Christ's Descent into Sheol   19

6   The Future of Hell   25

7   Paul Never Preaches Hell   27

8   Conclusion   33

CHAPTER 1

Why Study Hell?

Hell is one of the most misunderstood doctrines in Scripture. This confusion has led to countless misinterpretations about what hell is, where it is, who goes there, and why. Instead of turning to the Bible itself, many people, both inside and outside the church, have inherited ideas shaped more by tradition and imagination than by Scripture.

Two examples of works that have shaped the modern view of hell are Dante's Inferno and John Milton's Paradise Lost. Neither was intended as theological authority, yet both have profoundly influenced how people visualize hell. Each portrays demons ruling in hell, tormenting the souls of the damned. Satan is depicted in Paradise Lost as enthroned in this fiery domain, commanding his forces. These images, though dramatic and compelling as literature, are not drawn from Scripture. Yet they have been absorbed into our cultural understanding of hell.

Because of this, many popular ideas about hell today are built on fiction rather than fact. This leads to preaching that emphasizes fear, portraying the gospel primarily as an escape from hellfire. The message becomes one of "turn or burn," rather than an invitation into the joy, peace, and freedom found in a relationship with God.

The purpose of this study is to clear away those misconceptions and take a serious, literal look at what the Bible actually teaches about hell. To build an understanding of Hell based entirely on the text rather than any belief systems. By going back to Scripture, we can uncover the truth that has often been buried by tradition and cultural influence. The best place to start is with the first use of the word.

CHAPTER 2

THE FIRST MENTIONS

The English Word and the Original Word

The word *"hell"* first appears in the Bible in Deuteronomy 32:22: Which says *"For a fire is kindled in mine anger, and shall burn unto the lowest hell, and shall consume the earth with her increase, and set on fire the foundations of the mountains."* While this is technically the first English use of "hell," the verse does not reveal much about hell's nature or structure. It is not a doctrinal teaching about hell itself, but a declaration of judgment. God's fire burns to the "lowest hell," but the verse focuses on His judgment consuming the earth and shaking its foundations.

The best we can do here is look at the Hebrew word underlying the English word Hell, which is Sheol (לִֹשְאוֹל). This word is commonly translated as "grave" which is it's most literal understanding. From this perspective, the most straightforward reading of Deuteronomy 32:22 is that God's wrath reaches even to the deepest burial place, the very depths of the earth.

However, now that we are looking at the Hebrew word *Sheol*, we find that this is not its first appearance in Scripture. And that is where this study becomes much more revealing. In fact, the true first mention of Hell or *Sheol* in the Bible gives us a more insightful look into what the Old Testament writers believed about the condition of the dead. Which opens the door to a better understanding of what hell really is.

This is why it is important to consider the original Hebrew and Greek alongside the English. Relying on the English word *hell* alone would have caused us to miss the more revealing first use of *Sheol*, and with it, a clearer picture of what the biblical concept of hell is.

First Use in Hebrew

The first use of the Hebrew word Sheol in the Bible appears in Genesis 37:35, where Jacob mourns what he believes is the death of his son Joseph. You may know the context well: Joseph's brothers sold him into slavery, then deceived their father by bringing back Joseph's coat dipped in animal blood to make it appear he had been killed. Overcome with grief, Jacob refuses to be comforted and says, *"I will go down into the grave [Sheol] unto my son mourning."*

At this point in the account, Jacob believes Joseph is dead. Yet he has no body, no grave, and no evidence beyond a bloodied coat. This makes Jacob's statement

4

significant. When he says he will go down into the grave *unto* his son, he cannot mean burial in the same physical location as his son, because in Jacob's mind, Joseph's body is either destroyed or lost. When Jacob speaks of going "unto my son," he must mean something beyond the literal act of burial in a grave. The phrase reveals something deeper: Jacob believes that he and Joseph will be reunited in Sheol.

This passage offers early evidence that Sheol was understood not just as a grave or a resting place for the body, but as a place where the dead continued in some form of existence, and where reunion was possible. Jacob's hope is to join his son in the place where the dead are gathered.

A supporting example of this same expectation is found in 2 Samuel 12:23, after David loses his infant son. David says, *"But now he is dead, wherefore should I fast? can I bring him back again? I shall go to him, but he shall not return to me."* Like Jacob, David expresses a confident belief that he will one day be with his child again, not just in death, but with him in the place of the dead. This again suggests that Sheol, from the earliest references, was understood as a shared destination, where reunion with loved ones after death was expected.

Some may argue that these are simply poetic or grief-filled expressions, and that I am reading them too literally. But how often do parents grieving their recently deceased child break into poetic prose? The Bible records the words of Jacob and David fully and historically. To argue otherwise is to undermine the inerrancy of Scripture, a separate discussion entirely.

Furthermore, their language is relational and directional, it expresses their hope in dark and difficult moments. These are not vapid or empty expressions. Jacob and David, while dealing with their grief differently, both express their belief that they will go somewhere to be with their children.

CHAPTER 3

ALL THE DEAD WENT TO SHEOL

Another passage that reveals this biblical understanding of Sheol is found in Job 3:11–19. In the midst of his intense suffering and despair, Job curses the day of his birth and wishes that he had never been born. He reasons that if he had died in the womb or as an infant, he would now be at rest.

He says, *"Then had I been at rest, with kings and counsellors of the earth... There the wicked cease from troubling; and there the weary be at rest."* He continues, describing it as the place where prisoners are freed, the slave is no longer under his master, and the great and small alike are gathered together. This description makes it clear that Sheol was not understood only as a place of fiery torment, nor as a place reserved only for the wicked. Rather, it was the universal destination of the dead, both righteous and unrighteous.

Job, who is portrayed as a righteous man throughout the book, longs for Sheol because he views Sheol as a place of relief from suffering. He does not expect to be taken to heaven; instead, he expects, like everyone else, to go down into Sheol when he dies. That expectation does not diminish his righteousness; it reflects the prevailing understanding in the Old Testament that all the dead, both the wicked and the righteous, go to Sheol, which is hell.

Old Testament Believers Did Not Expect To Go To Heaven

Contrary to many modern assumptions, Old Testament believers did not believe they would go to heaven when they died. This was not only the understanding of Job, but of all the faithful from Genesis onward. Their hope was firmly rooted in the promise of a future resurrection, not in an immediate ascent to heaven. They understood death as a descent into Sheol, where they would wait until God fulfilled His promises to raise them again. Nowhere in the Old Testament do the righteous express a hope of going to live in heaven after death. Instead, they looked forward to God restoring them to life on the earth.

They Expected to Go to the Grave (Sheol) and Wait for the Resurrection

One clear example of this expectation comes from Isaiah 38, when King Hezekiah becomes deathly ill. In his prayer, he reflects on his condition and says, *"I shall go to the gates of the grave: I am deprived of the residue of my years."* He then adds, *"For the grave cannot praise thee, death can not celebrate thee: they that go down into the pit cannot hope for thy truth."* (Isaiah 38:10, 17–19). Hezekiah, though a righteous man and a king in good standing before God, did not expect to go to heaven or dwell in the presence of the Lord after death. He expected to go to the grave, Sheol, and there, as he says, no one could praise God as the living do. The living were those who could still make known God's truth to the next generation. This phrase, "the grave cannot praise thee", is a recurring concept in the Old Testament. It reflects a shared belief that Sheol was a realm of silence and waiting, not worship and communion with God.

This same expectation is echoed in the words of Job. In Job 14:10–14, he asks, *"Man dieth, and wasteth away... where is he?... O that thou wouldest hide me in the grave... keep me secret, until thy wrath be past... If a man die, shall he live again? all the days of my appointed time will I wait, till my change come."*

Job does not speak of heaven, nor of being in God's presence at death. Instead, he anticipates being hidden in the grave until the time of resurrection. He declares that he will wait until his "change" comes, showing a clear expectation of being raised again at some future time.

Both of these passages confirm that the Old Testament view of the afterlife was consistent: both the righteous and the wicked went to Sheol, and the righteous looked forward to a future resurrection, not a present heavenly reward.

CHAPTER 4

SHEOL / HADES: A DUAL REALM

As we continue developing a literal understanding of hell, Luke 16:22–26 becomes one of the most significant passages to examine. Jesus tells the account of a rich man and a beggar named Lazarus, both of whom die and enter into two very different experiences in the afterlife. In the Greek, the word Jesus uses for Hell in this passage is Ἅιδης, or Hades and is the Greek equivalent to Sheol.

It is important to note that Sheol, Hades, and Hell are words from different languages that refer to the same place. I have been using Sheol and Hell somewhat interchangeably because Sheol is the Hebrew word translated as "Hell" in the KJV. Sheol does not appear in most English Bibles and carries the literal meaning of "grave," so it is sometimes translated that way. The Greek word Hades is the New Testament equivalent of Sheol and Hell, and it too is occasionally translated as "grave." Even though these words can literally mean grave, the context determines whether the text refers to a burial place or to the waiting place of the dead.

Some scholars, such as E.W. Bullinger, interpret Luke 16:22-26 as a parable. However, it does not meet the biblical criteria for a parable and therefore should be understood as a literal historical account that Christ is relaying.

Jesus himself defined the purpose of parables in Mark 4:11–12, saying, *"Unto you it is given to know the mystery of the kingdom of God: but unto them that are without, all these things are done in parables."* A parable is a veiled story that reveals a mystery of the kingdom to some while concealing it from others. But in Luke 16, the subject is not the kingdom. The story is neither symbolic nor allegorical in tone. Instead, it plainly describes what happens to the righteous and the unrighteous immediately after death. Nothing in the passage suggests Jesus is masking deeper truths behind metaphor. Rather, He is revealing something previously veiled about the state of the dead.

What this passage shows is that Hell is not a single and equal repository of the dead. Rather a place with two distinct compartments: one of comfort and rest, where Lazarus is taken, often referred to as "Abraham's bosom", and another of torment and flame, where the rich man finds himself. These two regions are separated by what the text calls a "great gulf" While odd in the English the Greek word used here is χάσμα (chasma) you may be able to guess the meaning from that, it means a chasm, gulf, or pit. This clarifies that the rich man is not looking upward toward heaven, but rather across a massive divide within Sheol itself.

This passage provides the clearest and most comprehensive description of hell found anywhere in the Bible. It reveals that Sheol is not only a place of fire and agony, but also a place of comfort and peace, depending on which side one is found. Even though Luke 16 gives the most detailed account of this structure, the concept is not technically new. Multiple Old Testament passages allude to it, though those references are more scattered throughout Scripture.

For example, Isaiah 57:1–2 speaks of the righteous dying and entering into rest: *"He shall enter into peace: they shall rest in their beds, each one walking in his uprightness."* In contrast, Psalm 49:14 speaks of the fate of the wicked: *"Like sheep they are laid in the grave; death shall feed on them... their beauty shall consume in the grave from their dwelling."* The wicked are consumed in Sheol, while the righteous rest, clear evidence of two separate experiences within the same place of the dead.

What Is the Pit?

Now, besides Paradise and Torment, the Great Gulf which we determined to be a chasm, may also be another compartment of Hell. The fact that it is a chasm leads us naturally into a deeper biblical concept: the Pit, a term that is often used in association with Hell. One such example comes from the passage used earlier of king Hezekiah, where he says" *For the grave cannot praise thee, death can not celebrate thee: they that go down into the pit cannot hope for thy truth.*" Throughout scripture the pit is often mentioned alongside Hell, I will now present that the Pit and the Chasm from Luke 16 are the same thing.

The Greek word ἄβυσσος (*abyssos*), translated as "bottomless pit," appears repeatedly in the New Testament, especially in prophetic and apocalyptic passages, it appears to be a special prison, reserved for certain fallen angels to be kept until judgment.

As is seen in Revelation 9:1–2, where during the trumpet judgments, a star falls from heaven and is given the key to the bottomless pit. When it is opened, smoke arises as from a great furnace, and out of it comes a demonic horde. These supernatural beings were locked away and only released to judge the earth.

This is alluded to in 2 Peter 2:4, which says, *"God spared not the angels that sinned, but cast them down to hell, and delivered them into chains of darkness, to be reserved unto judgment."* The word translated "hell" here is Tartarus, used only once in the New Testament, and refers specifically to this place of confinement.

The role of the pit is especially important when we consider the fate of Satan himself. In Isaiah 14:9–15, a prophetic taunt is directed at the king of Babylon, but clearly extends to Satan. It reads, *"Hell from beneath is moved for thee to meet thee at thy coming... thou shalt be brought down to hell, to the sides of the pit."* This prophecy places Satan not only in hell, but specifically in the sides of the pit.

This prophecy will find its fulfillment in Revelation 20:1–3, where an angel descends from heaven with the key to the bottomless pit and a great chain. He seizes the dragon, that old serpent called the Devil and Satan, and casts him into the Abyss, where he is shut up and sealed for a thousand years. This period of imprisonment matches the prophecy of Isaiah: Satan is brought low, confined in the pit, awaiting a final fate. After a thousand years, he is released for a short season and then cast into the Lake of Fire, a separate, final place of eternal punishment. This distinction is important because hell itself is later thrown into the Lake of Fire (Revelation 20:14). Therefore, the Lake cannot simply be "hell"; as such, the prophecy of Isaiah 14 cannot be fulfilled by casting Satan into the Lake of Fire. So then, the Abyss, the bottomless pit, is a part of Hell, it is the prison for the spirits, it is the great gulf fixed between Paradise and Torment.

Hell Is a Physical Location in the Earth

Having connected the concept of the pit to Sheol, we now turn to one of the more dramatic events in the Old Testament to demonstrate that hell should be understood as a physical location within the earth. In Numbers 16:30–33, during the rebellion of Korah, the Lord performs a supernatural judgment. Moses declares that if the earth opens and swallows these men alive, it will be a sign that they have provoked the Lord. The text records exactly that: *"The earth opened her mouth, and swallowed them up... and they went down alive into the pit."*

15

This phrase, *"alive into the pit,"* is deliberate. It is not poetic language. These men did not die and then fall into Hell; rather, the earth itself opened beneath them, and they descended alive into "the pit", a term we have linked with Sheol, and the abyss. That detail, that they went down *alive,* strongly implies they were not yet dead when they entered hell, it raises the serious possibility that the pit and hell is not just a spiritual realm, but a literal, physical location within the earth.

Further support for this interpretation is found in Psalm 88, a psalm written for the sons of Korah. Uniquely, this psalm is written from the perspective of someone who appears to be conscious in the pit. The writer says in verse 3, *"For my soul is full of troubles: and my life draweth nigh unto the grave."* He continues in verses 4–6, *"I am counted with them that go down into the pit... thou hast laid me in the lowest pit, in darkness, in the deeps."* The language is not of final death, but of a living soul overwhelmed and surrounded by death, in "the lowest pit." If this is intended as a reflection on Korah's rebellion and those swallowed into the earth, then it reinforces the idea that they descended alive and consciously into Sheol.

Additional support comes from other Old Testament passages that speak of hell as being located downward, inside the earth. In Ezekiel 31:14–17, a prophetic lament describes mighty nations being brought low, with this statement: *"They also went down into hell with him unto them that be slain with the sword."* The descent is downward, not metaphorical, but directional. Similarly, in Amos 9:2, God says of those who would seek to escape His judgment,

"Though they dig into hell, thence shall mine hand take them." Again, the language speaks of hell being within the earth, something that could be "dug into."

Taken together, these verses build a consistent picture. Hell, Sheol, the pit, the abyss, these are not ethereal, spiritual realms. The biblical authors understood hell as a real, physical place, deep within the earth itself. It was the realm where all the dead went: righteous, unrighteous, and, in rare and dramatic cases like Korah, the living swallowed into it by direct judgment from God.

CHAPTER 5

CHRIST'S DESCENT INTO SHEOL

Jesus Descended into the Lower Parts of the Earth

The death and resurrection of Christ involved not only the cross and the empty tomb, but also a descent into the deepest pit of the earth. Scripture plainly teaches that after His death, Christ went not to heaven, but to the place of the dead, where He proclaimed His victory.

In 1 Peter 3:18–20, Peter writes, *"Being put to death in the flesh, but quickened by the Spirit: by which also he went and preached unto the spirits in prison; which sometime were disobedient..."* This passage tells us that after Christ was "put to death in the flesh," He was "quickened," that is, made alive, "by the Spirit." In that spiritual state, before His bodily resurrection, Christ went and preached to spirits in prison. These spirits are said to have been disobedient in the days of Noah, which closely aligns with the imprisoned angels mentioned in 2 Peter 2:4 and Jude 6, those that were cast into *Tartarus,* or the pit, and "reserved in chains under darkness." The word "preached" here is not the usual term for preaching the gospel (*euangelizō*), but rather *kērussō* (κηρύσσω), which means to proclaim or herald. Christ was not evangelizing; He was announcing His triumph.

This descent is confirmed by Ephesians 4:9, which says, *"Now that he ascended, what is it but that he also descended first into the lower parts of the earth?"* The phrase "lower parts of the earth" is not figurative; it refers to what we have already demonstrated from Scripture: Sheol, or Hades, the place of the dead, located in the earth. More specifically, the term aligns with the lowest compartment, the pit, where the imprisoned spirits reside. This descent must have occurred before Christ ascended into heaven. Therefore, Christ's journey was not immediately upward upon death, but downward, into Sheol, to declare His authority over death, sin, and the spiritual powers He had defeated.

In Romans 10:6–7, Paul rhetorically asks, *"Who shall descend into the deep? (that is, to bring up Christ again from the dead)".* The word translated "deep" here is the Greek *abyssos* (ἄβυσσος), the same word used elsewhere in the New Testament to describe the bottomless pit, found in Revelation 9:1–2, Revelation 11:7, and Revelation 20:1–3. This is not general language for the grave; it refers specifically to the lowest region of Sheol/Hades, the prison of spirits and fallen angels.

The fact that Paul uses this same term to describe where Christ was before rising again from the dead makes it clear that Jesus did not only go to the comfort side (Paradise) of Sheol; He descended to the lowest regions, into the Abyss. This completes the picture: Christ did not merely die; He entered the realm of the dead, to Paradise to comfort the righteous, and to the Pit to proclaim His victory over sin, death, and all the powers of darkness.

Jesus Did Not Go to Heaven That Day

In Luke 23:43, as Jesus hangs on the cross, He turns to the believing thief beside Him and says, *"Verily I say unto thee, Today shalt thou be with me in paradise."* Many assume this to mean that Jesus and the thief went to heaven that day. However, Jesus did not say "heaven." He said "paradise," and there is good biblical reason to understand this paradise as Abraham's Bosom, the place of comfort in Sheol, where the righteous dead awaited resurrection.

This interpretation is supported by the account in Luke 16:22–23. The "bosom of Abraham" is not Heaven, but the resting place of the righteous dead, distinct from the place of torment, yet still located within Sheol (or Hades).

Further confirmation comes from John 20:17, when the resurrected Christ tells Mary Magdalene, *"Touch me not; for I am not yet ascended to my Father."* This occurs after His death and resurrection, which means that Jesus had not yet been to Heaven, even days after His statement to the thief. This proves beyond doubt that whatever "Paradise" was, it was not Heaven.

Putting the pieces together, it becomes clear: after His death, Jesus descended into Sheol, to the paradise side, where the believing thief would also go. From there, He preached to the spirits in prison and declared His victory. Only after this descent and His resurrection would He ascend bodily to the Father in Heaven.

Did Jesus Empty Sheol or Take the Righteous to Heaven?

A common teaching suggests that when Jesus rose from the dead, He emptied Abraham's Bosom (the comfort side of Sheol) and took the righteous dead to heaven. However, this idea, though widespread, has no scriptural support. Nowhere does the Bible say that Abraham's Bosom or Paradise was emptied, dismantled, or vacated after Christ's resurrection. No passage ever describes the righteous dead being transferred from Sheol to heaven.

This belief is often linked to Ephesians 4:8, which says, *"When he ascended up on high, he led captivity captive, and gave gifts unto men."* Many take this to mean that Jesus freed the righteous from Sheol and brought them to heaven. However, a close reading of the passage reveals that this interpretation is not supported by the text itself. The verse says nothing about Sheol, Hades, Paradise, or Abraham's Bosom. Instead, the word "captivity" must be understood contextually.

There is strong reason to believe that the "captivity" Christ took captive is not the souls of the dead but rather sin itself. Throughout Paul's letters, sin is described as a power that held mankind captive (cf. Romans 7:23, Galatians 3:22). Christ, through His death and resurrection, broke the chains of that captivity, not by emptying the underworld, but by defeating sin's dominion over mankind and offering justification by faith.

Furthermore, as we have shown, Christ did not ascend to Heaven until after His resurrection, and the forty days following. Therefore, Christ could not have taken the righteous dead to heaven until then. However, Christ's ascension is singular; He goes alone up to His Father, and there is no mention of the dead ascending with Him. Outside of Ephesians 4:8, there is not even a hint that Hell is emptied, which we have shown is a very loose connection on its own.

Thus, the triumph described in Ephesians 4 is not the emptying of Sheol, but the leading of a spiritual victory procession, in which the very thing that once enslaved us, sin is now conquered and led in defeat.

CHAPTER 6

THE FUTURE OF HELL

A Temporary Holding Place

As we near the conclusion of this study, it is important to understand that Hell is not the final destination for the souls of the dead. Instead, it serves as a temporary holding place, where both the righteous and the unrighteous await their respective resurrections.

For the righteous, Sheol was a place of rest and peace. Throughout the Old Testament, we have seen that those who walked uprightly before God expected to go to Sheol. They believed that they would wait for God's appointed day of resurrection. This is reflected in passages like Job 14:14, where Job says, *"All the days of my appointed time will I wait, till my change come."* This aligns with Daniel 12:2, which speaks of those who *"sleep in the dust of the earth"* awakening, some to everlasting life.

In contrast, the unrighteous experience Sheol or Hades as a place of torment. As Jesus described in Luke 16, the rich man was in torment while awaiting final judgment. His cry for relief reveals that the punishment had already begun, but the verdict was not yet complete. He, too, was awaiting resurrection, not to life, but to damnation (cf. John 5:29).

The final destination of hell is revealed in Revelation 20:13–14, which says, *"And the sea gave up the dead which were in it; and death and hell delivered up the dead which were in them... And death and hell were cast into the lake of fire. This is the second death."* This is the moment where Sheol is emptied, its purpose completed. The dead are judged, and then hell itself is cast into the Lake of Fire.

This is a critical distinction. Hell (Hades/Sheol) is not eternal, it is temporary. It holds the dead until the time appointed for them to stand before God. But the Lake of Fire is final. It is the second death, the place of eternal separation and judgment.

CHAPTER 7

PAUL NEVER PREACHES HELL, SO WHY DO WE?

A Call to Preach Grace as Grace Was Given

Now we move on to why this is mostly educational on what Hell is and not a missive on why you should be afraid of Hell.

Paul, the apostle to the Gentiles, our apostle, who was given the dispensation of the grace of God (Ephesians 3:1-12), only uses the word "Hell" once in any of his recorded sermons in the book of Acts or in all thirteen of his epistles. This absence is striking, especially when compared to the emphasis modern preaching often places on hellfire and eternal torment. Today, hell is frequently at the forefront of gospel presentations, used to stir fear and manipulate emotions. Yet Paul, the man entrusted with the message of grace for this current age, did not use the fear of hell to compel belief.

Paul Preaches Christ, Not Condemnation

Paul's gospel message was not built on threats of eternal punishment, but on the proclamation of a crucified and risen Christ. In 1 Corinthians 1:23–24, he writes, *"But we preach Christ crucified... Christ the power of God, and the wisdom of God."* His focus was never on where sinners would go if they rejected Christ, but on who Christ is and what He has done to reconcile the world to God. In 2 Corinthians 5:18–19, Paul declares that God has given us *"the ministry of reconciliation"* and is *not imputing trespasses unto the world.* This is not a message of wrath, but of peace and pardon.

Paul does not use fear of hell to drive people to the cross. Instead, he offers something far better: peace with God (Romans 5:1), justification by faith (Romans 5:9), and a gift of God, which is eternal life through Jesus Christ our Lord (Romans 6:23) His gospel is not centered on escaping hell, but on receiving eternal life, a life rooted in the finished work of Christ.

Paul makes the nature of salvation abundantly clear in Ephesians 2:8–9: *"For by grace are ye saved through faith; and that not of yourselves: it is the gift of God: not of works, lest any man should boast."* Again in Romans 6:14, he reminds believers, *"Ye are not under the law, but under grace."* There is no room for coercion in such a message, no place for fear-based appeals to eternal torment. If Paul is indeed our pattern, as he exhorts in 1 Corinthians 11:1 and Philippians 3:17, where twice he says "be followers of me," then preaching hellfire as a tool for evangelism is not Pauline.

The One Time Paul Mentions the Grave

Even though the word *Hell* never appears in English in any of Paul's writings, he does use the Greek word Hades, the same word translated as *Hell* elsewhere. But when Paul uses it, it is not in a warning or threat of punishment. Instead, it appears in a passage of triumph. In 1 Corinthians 15:55–57, Paul writes, *"O death, where is thy sting? O grave, where is thy victory? The sting of death is sin; and the strength of sin is the law. But thanks be to God, which giveth us the victory through our Lord Jesus Christ."* The word translated *"grave"* is Hades in Greek, and here Paul uses it not to threaten the lost, but to celebrate the ultimate future victory over death and hell.

This is not a fearful warning of judgment, but a bold declaration that both death and Hades will one day be entirely defeated. Though death and hell have not yet been cast into the Lake of Fire, Paul speaks as one already victorious. Those who are in Christ have no fear of the grave, because it has no claim on them. They are heaven-bound, and hell will never touch them. For to be absent from the body is to be present with the lord, who is in heaven at the right hand of God.

Some may argue that this is an "argument from silence." However, this ignores the progressive nature of Scripture that this book assumes. They may say, "Paul did not address polygamy directly; shall we treat silence

29

as endorsement?" But this book is not saying we should ignore the whole testimony of Scripture. Rather, I am showing that the message changed with Paul. Paul does not need to address every single topic. What matters is that he addresses hell once, pronouncing victory over it in Christ. This change in messaging should be normative, because Paul received a new message, as he says in Ephesians 3.

Preaching Fear vs. Preaching Peace

Paul's writings are unmistakably clear, the gospel he preached is one of peace, liberty, and assurance, not fear. In Romans 5:1, he proclaims, *"Therefore being justified by faith, we have peace with God through our Lord Jesus Christ."* This peace is not something earned, nor is it maintained through obedience; it is the immediate result of justification by faith.

In Galatians 5:1, Paul urges believers to *"Stand fast therefore in the liberty wherewith Christ hath made us free, and be not entangled again with the yoke of bondage."* To preach fear of hell as a motivation for faith is to return to a yoke of bondage, to the law, to condemnation and doubt. It clouds the very liberty Christ has purchased. But to preach grace, as Paul did, is to reflect the full peace and liberty made available through the cross.

This free gift, of righteousness and eternal life, of freedom and completeness in Christ, is available to anyone that would believe that Jesus, the son of God, died on the cross, was buried, and rose again.

CHAPTER 8

CONCLUSION

As we bring this study to a close, the picture that emerges is far different from the fiery throne rooms and mythic horrors that have dominated Western conceptions of Hell. Through a careful, literal reading of Scripture (guided by the words themselves, in Hebrew and Greek) we have uncovered the biblical identity of Hell: a real place, within the earth, known first as Sheol and later as Hades, now as Hell. It is the temporary abode of all the dead, both righteous and unrighteous, containing within it both rest and torment, divided by a great gulf, and structured not by myth or medieval invention but by divine revelation.

Sheol, Hades, and Hell are not separate concepts but linguistic equivalents from Hebrew, Greek, and English. They all refer to the same waiting place of the dead. From Jacob's expectation of reuniting with his son in Sheol, to David's confidence that he would again be with his child, to Job's desire to rest from suffering in the grave (we see that Old Testament believers did not anticipate going to heaven but instead to a shared place of the dead). Jesus Himself affirmed this reality in Luke 16, where He gives a literal account of two men in Sheol: one comforted, the other tormented, separated by a great gulf. This is the clearest view of Hell in Scripture (not speculation, but revealed truth).

We have also seen that this place includes the abyss (the pit) reserved for fallen angels and, ultimately, Satan himself. This pit is not myth or metaphor. It is a prison, within Hell, deep in the earth, where even Satan will be bound during the thousand-year reign. Hell is not Satan's throne; it is his judgment.

Yet Hell is not the final destination. Scripture is clear: death and Hell will be emptied and judged, and then cast into the Lake of Fire. This marks the second death, the final separation from God. Hell is temporary; the Lake of Fire is eternal.

Most importantly, we've discovered that Paul (the apostle to the Gentiles and the one entrusted with the gospel of grace) never preaches Hell as a motivator for faith. He mentions it only once, and even then, in victory. Paul's message is not "turn or burn," but "Christ crucified," the free gift of eternal life, the ministry of reconciliation. His gospel centers not on fear but on peace, liberty, and assurance through faith. To preach fear is to return to bondage. To preach grace is to follow Paul as he followed Christ.

Hell, according to Scripture, is real. But so is the victory over it. For the believer today, death is not a descent into Sheol (it is to be present with the Lord). And this is the hope we preach: not fear, but freedom; not torment, but triumph; not judgment, but Jesus.

ABOUT THE AUTHOR

Dr. Randy White writes:

Luca Welch is my current intern in a program I have used for fifteen years to train young men for ministry. The heart of this program is not merely academic work, but the cultivation of the mind. Interns learn to read the Scriptures literally, to think outside the box, and to discipline themselves to write their material so others may benefit from it.

Luca, age twenty-three, comes from Smithville, Missouri. He possesses a sharp mind and a well-honed analytical ability, and he brings real hope for the future of what I call "thinking and theological pastors." This volume stands as the first of what I hope will be many theological works from Luca Welch.

To learn more about the intern program with Randy White Ministries, contact:

randy@randywhiteministries.org